TANTRI THE MANTRI

Script: Appaswami
Illustrations: Ashok Dongre

HEY! WHAT'S THIS? A TOY HORSE?

THIS IS A FLYING HORSE, SIR.

HA!

HOW CAN AN IRON HORSE FLY?

IT CAN, SIR.

COME BACK IN TWO DAYS AND SEE FOR YOURSELF!

WHY NOT NOW?

RIGHT NOW, IT CAN FLY LIKE A BIRD...

5

Changing Times

In the two decades from 1984 to 2004 several artists and writers worked on the Tantri series at different times. Ajit Vasaikar who succeeded Dongre as artist shared Shakespeare's view that villains should have a 'lean and hungry look'. He changed Tantri's appearance beyond recognition, turning him into a beanpole. Hooja took on a beefy appearance and lost his air of innocence. The next artist, Anand Mande, continued in the same vein, but gave both men longer, fleshier noses and better headgear.

Another radical change in the physical appearance of the protagonists occurred towards the end of the 1990s when Savio Mascarenhas became the main artist for the series. Savio gave both Tantri and Hooja a facelift, and reduced the difference in their heights to practically nil. Savio had other commitments and was pressed for time, especially when he started illustrating the Shikari Shambu comics episodes. In 2000, the editors decided to hand over the responsibility of illustrating the Tantri series to Prachi Killekar. Prachi made a faltering start, confused by the different representations of Hooja and Tantri she had to choose from, but eventually came up with their present forms.

She continues to be the illustrator for the series.

Ashok Dongre

Ajit Vasaikar

Anand Mande

Savio Mascarenhas

But, the theme remained the same:

WHY DOESN'T HE DROP DEAD! I WANT TO BE KING!!!

I'M FORTUNATE TO HAVE SUCH A LOYAL AND DEVOTED MANTRI!

WRITERS

Many of the Tantri episodes are based on stories sent by Tinkle readers. But quite a few are written by professional comics writers – among them, Prasad Iyer, Luis Fernandes, Alok Mathur, Reena Puri, and in recent times, Rajani Thindiath and R. Nalini.

TANTRI THE MANTRI

UMBRELLA!

Based on a story sent by:
Amol Ashok Gopale,
Mumbai - 400 022.

Illustrations :
Prachi Killekar

IT WAS A DARK AND GLOOMY DAY...

...BUT TANTRI'S MOOD WAS DARKER AND GLOOMIER.

WHY! WHY! WHY!...

...WHY CAN'T HOOJA JUST BE STRUCK BY LIGHTNING!

WELL...TANTRI SURE HAD BEEN STRUCK BY SOMETHING.

DUSHTABUDDHI! I WANT YOU TO MAKE... AN UMBRELLA THAT ATTRACTS LIGHTNING!

OOO! AN EVIL SCHEME FOR AN EVIL MIND.

9

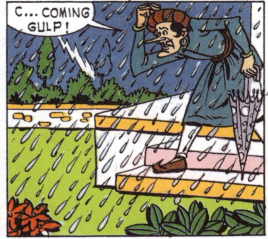

11

TANTRI THE MANTRI

Coconut Bomb

Based on a story sent by:
H. S. Vinay.

Illustrations :
Prachi Killekar

AH ! WHAT A BEAUTIFUL SCENE. WISH I COULD PUSH RAJA HOOJA OFF ONE OF THESE MOUNTAINS.

I WISH SOMEBODY COULD COME UP WITH A FOOLPROOF PLAN TO PUSH RAJA HOOJA OFF THE THRONE.

HERE I AM!

IT WAS DHOOM, THE MAGICIAN.

DHOOM, WHAT BRINGS YOU HERE TODAY ?

ANOTHER MISCHIEF. BEHOLD! A COCONUT BOMB !

FOR A HUNDRED GOLD COINS, YOU CAN BLOW THE KING UP.

HMM... NOT BAD. I'LL TAKE IT.

TANTRI DIRECTLY WENT TO THE KING'S PALACE AND FOUND HIM STROLLING IN THE GARDEN.

HERE'S MY CHANCE ! I'LL JUST THROW IT ON HIM.

BEFORE YOU ADDRESS THE GATHERING, WHY DON'T YOU BREAK THE COCONUT? IT'LL BE AN AUSPICIOUS BEGINNING.

HA HA! TANTRI, I NEVER KNEW YOU'D BE SO SUPERSTITIOUS. LET'S JUST GET ON WITH THE FEAST.

DRAT! ANOTHER PLAN DOWN THE DRAIN. WHEN WILL I MANAGE TO GET RID OF THIS FATSO?

LATER, IN HIS CHAMBER, AN IDEA STRUCK HIM.

AH! YES! TO REACH THE PALACE EARLY IN THE MORNING AND MY WORK'S AS GOOD AS DONE.

THE NEXT MORNING —

IS THE KING AWAKE?

YES, HE IS SITTING AT HIS MORNING PRAYERS.

INSIDE —

GOOD MORNING! NICE WAY TO START THE DAY!

HELLO! COME AND JOIN ME.

YES, I'M COMING. I HAVE A COCONUT WITH ME. THE GODS WOULD BLESS YOU AND OUR KINGDOM IF YOU OFFER THIS.

GOOD IDEA! BRING THE COCONUT OVER.

14

TANTRI THE MANTRI
THE RECORD RUN

Based on a story sent by: Sanjay B. Kulkarni,

Illustrations : Prachi Killekar

AT THE ANNUAL SPORTS MEET HOSTED BY KING SUMANTRA OF SUMANTRAPUR—

THE RESULTS BEFORE OUR LAST EVENT ARE: KING ZORAWAR'S TEAM: 20 POINTS AND A TIE BETWEEN KING HOOJA'S TEAM AND KING SUMANTRA'S TEAM, BOTH AT 35 POINTS!

THE FINAL EVENT WAS A 100-METRE RACE.

WITH THE CHAMPION SPRINTER, MAKHAN SINGH, ON OUR TEAM. WE WILL SURELY WIN.

I'M CONFIDENT THAT MY MEN WILL TAKE THE TROPHY HOME.

I BET ONE QUARTER OF MY KINGDOM ON MY VICTORY.

DONE! WHOEVER LOSES THE RACE, LOSES A QUARTER OF HIS KINGDOM TO THE WINNER.

ONE OF HOOJA'S MINISTERS WAS STANDING NEARBY.

WHAT HAVE YOU DONE, SIRE? MAKHAN SINGH IS UNBEATABLE.

OOPS! IS THAT SO?...

...WHERE'S TANTRI? I'M SURE HE'D FIND A WAY OUT.

16

17

THE MAN OUTSIDE WAS ALERT TO THE SIGNAL. HE IMMEDIATELY SHOT THE ARROW.

THE ARROW SWIFTLY FOLLOWED THE FLOWER IN THE GARLAND.

MAKHAN SINGH IS TRYING HARD TO MATCH TANTRI'S SPEED...

BRAVO, TANTRI!

...HE'S LEFT MAKHAN SINGH WAY BEHIND..NO DOUBT ABOUT THE WINNER!

FASTER.. FASTER.

THE ARROW TOO WAS GAINING SPEED.

IT CAME DANGEROUSLY CLOSE WHEN —

I'M FINISHED.. BUT WHY AM I HOLDING ON TO THIS WRETCHED GARLAND? IT IS THIS THAT THE ARROW IS FOLLOWING....

TANTRI TANTRI

HE FLUNG THE GARLAND AWAY AND ...

...REACHED THE FINISHING LINE.

THE WINNER IS TANTRI, FROM HOOJA'S TEAM.

OH! THERE GOES A QUARTER OF MY KINGDOM.

YAY!

SEE HOW WELL THE GOOD-LUCK CHARM WORKED!

?

TANTRI THE MANTRI

VALIANT HOOJA

Story :
S. Charulatha

Script :
Reena I. Puri

Illustrations :
Prachi Killekar

TANTRI WAS PAYING A SECRET VISIT TO KING DAMRU'S COURT.

....SO IF THAT PODGY KING OF YOURS CAN BE REMOVED, I WILL CROWN YOU KING AND RULE THROUGH YOU.

SUITS ME FINE.

HERE WAS ANOTHER EXCELLENT PLOT TO OVERTHROW KING HOOJA.

KING DAMRU DECLARED WAR ON HOOJA'S KINGDOM.

DAMRU HAS WRITTEN THAT PEOPLE WITH FAT BELLIES SHOULD BE COOKS AND NOT KINGS.

WHAT AN INSULT, YOUR MAJESTY! YOU MUST LEAD US TO WAR.

LEAD! I COULD ALWAYS SUPERVISE FROM THE BACK.

NO, SIRE. A KING MUST LEAD.

HOOJA HAD TO AGREE. BUT LATER —

TANTRI, YOU MUST BE WITH ME ALL THE TIME, YOU ARE MY GOOD LUCK CHARM.

B..BUT, SIRE ....

NO 'BUTS', YOU WILL SIT BY ME IN THE HOWDAH*

* DECORATED SEAT ON TOP OF AN ELEPHANT.

20

KING DAMRU ATTACKED THE NEXT MORNING.

WHY DID HE HAVE TO ATTACK SO EARLY?

HE LIKES TO FINISH ALL HIS OUTDOOR WORK BY LUNCH TIME.

KING HOOJA'S ARMY FOUGHT BRAVELY.

TAKE THAT, YOU BIG APE!

AAAOOOOOOO

BOINK

THUNK

THUD

DAMRU SAW HOOJA ON HIS ELEPHANT AND AIMED AT HIM.

OOOOK! DAMRU IS GOING TO SHOOT ME.

SAVE ME, DEAR TANTRI.

UH!

THE ARROW CAME WHIZZING AND —

HELP!

UNGH!

21

TANTRI COLLAPSED IN A HEAP.

OH NO! TANTRI, MY DEAR FELLOW! OPEN YOUR EYES.

SLAP SLAP

CALL THE PHYSICIAN!

IN A MOMENT, SIRE.. E..EEEE.

BONK

HE IS LOSING BLOOD. HOW DARE THAT WRETCHED DAMRU SHOOT MY LOYAL MANTRI.

A STRANGE KIND OF ANGER FILLED KING HOOJA, AND —

MURDERER! THUG! DACOIT!

HOOJA RAN STRAIGHT TO DAMRU.

I'LL GET YOU!

SIT DOWN, YOU POMPOUS PACHYDERM.

THE ELEPHANT WAS IMPRESSED AND PROMPTLY SAT DOWN.

GET UP, YOU DEVIOUS DAMRU...

...LET ME BONK YOUR DUMB FACE.

BONK BONK

KING DAMRU COLLAPSED OUT OF SHEER FRIGHT...

GOOD FIGHT.

BRAVO! BRAVO!

SOLID PUNCH!

...AND VALIANT HOOJA CARRIED HIM AWAY AS BOOTY.

NO ONE TOUCHES MY TANTRI AND GETS AWAY WITH IT.

CLAP

CLAP

CLAP

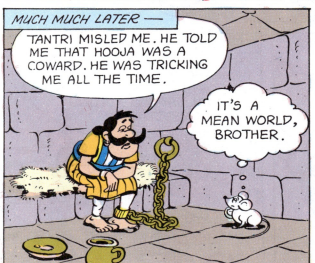

MUCH MUCH LATER —

TANTRI MISLED ME. HE TOLD ME THAT HOOJA WAS A COWARD. HE WAS TRICKING ME ALL THE TIME.

IT'S A MEAN WORLD, BROTHER.

IN ANOTHER PART OF THE PALACE—

....AND THEN THE KING JUMPED OFF HIS ELEPHANT AND....

SHEESH! THAT'S THE 104TH TIME I AM HEARING THE STORY.

TANTRI THE MANTRI
THE KILLER LADDOO

Based on a story sent by : H. S. Pranav.

Illustrations : Prachi Killekar

IT WAS DIWALI BUT TANTRI WAS GLUM.

I WISH HOOJA'S HEAD WAS A LADDOO. THEN I COULD ROLL IT DOWN A HILL. SIGH! I GUESS I'LL JUST EAT IT UP FOR NOW!

BUT —

STOP! DON'T. THIS IS NO ORDINARY LADDOO. IT IS THE LADDOO OF YOUR DREAMS.

WH.. WHO'S THAT?

IT WAS DUSHTABUDDHI.

DUSHTABUDDHI! WHAT IS SO SPECIAL ABOUT IT?

IT IS TIGHTLY PACKED WITH SODIUM. THE MINUTE IT COMES IN CONTACT WITH WATER OR SALIVA IT WILL BURST...

...AND IT IS YOURS FOR ONLY 200 GOLD COINS.

NOT SO FAST, MY FRIEND. YOU WILL GET YOUR PAYMENT ONLY AFTER THIS WORKS.

HOOJA, HERE I COME.

UH, HUH!

AT HOOJA'S PALACE —

AH! TANTRI. JUST THE MAN I WANTED TO SEE. WILL YOU BE ONE OF THE JUDGES FOR THE ANNUAL LADDOO-EATING COMPETITION?

HEH! HEH! WITH PLEASURE, SIRE.

WAIT TILL YOU EAT MY LADDOO, PUDDING FACE.

MEANWHILE IN RAJA DOOJA'S PALACE —

BRING ME HOOJA'S HEAD THIS TIME. AND DON'T BUNGLE IT.

MY GIGANTIC LADDOO WILL NOT MISS. WE'LL GET HIM ON THE DAY OF THE LADDOO-EATING COMPETITION.

THE DAY OF THE COMPETITION DAWNED BRIGHT AND CLEAR.

TANTRI, THE AROMA OF LADDOOS IS KILLING ME. I TOO WILL PARTICIPATE IN THE COMPETITION.

BUT.. SIRE, HOW CAN YOU?

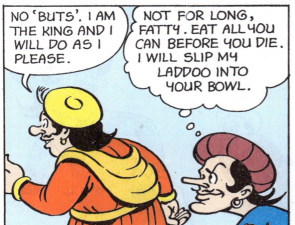

NO 'BUTS'. I AM THE KING AND I WILL DO AS I PLEASE.

NOT FOR LONG, FATTY. EAT ALL YOU CAN BEFORE YOU DIE. I WILL SLIP MY LADDOO INTO YOUR BOWL.

BUT —

HEY, WHERE ARE YOU TAKING ME? I WANT TO GO WITH RAJA HOOJA.

TANTRIJI, SINCE YOU ARE A JUDGE, YOU MUST SIT IN OUR SPECIAL SEAT. NEITHER YOU NOR ANYBODY ELSE WILL BE ALLOWED NEAR THE PARTICIPANTS.

I WILL HAVE TO FEED HIM THE LADDOO AFTER THE COMPETITION.

THIS IS THE MOST EXCITING LADDOO-EATING COMPETITION EVER. RAJA HOOJA AND KHATERAHO ARE THE ONLY TWO LEFT.

KHATERAHO HAS GAINED THE LEAD. RAJA HOOJA LOOKS ILL.

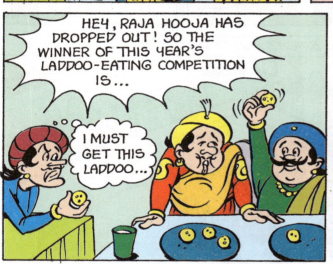

HEY, RAJA HOOJA HAS DROPPED OUT! SO THE WINNER OF THIS YEAR'S LADDOO-EATING COMPETITION IS...

I MUST GET THIS LADDOO...

...KHATERAHO!

...TO HOOJA.

SIRE, I HAVE KEPT THIS SPECIAL LADDOO FOR YOU...

BELCH! TANTRI, I AM ILL. I HAVE EATEN TOO MANY LADDOOS. YOU..GAK.. MUST GIVE AWAY THE PRIZE. I AM GOING BACK TO REST. OOOGH!

BAH! JUST MY LUCK. I WILL HAVE TO WAIT TO GIVE HIM THIS LADDOO.

TANTRIJI, PLEASE COME ON THE STAGE.

26

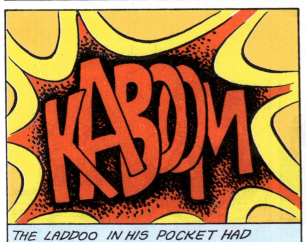

TANTRI THE MANTRI
'THE PITFALL'

Based on a story sent by: D. Rakesh, Illustrations: Prachi Killekar

EVERYONE IN HOOJA'S KINGDOM SEEMED TO WANT TO BECOME FIT AND STRONG.

101, 102, 103....

HEY! MOVE OVER AND GIVE ME SOME SPACE.

MORE SPACE?

EVERYONE FROM THE SOLDIERS...

ATTENTION!

HUP, 1, 2, 3... HUP, 1, 2, 3....

...TO THE PRISONERS...

THERE, STRETCH.. ST..R..E..T..CH.

OOOH!

AH!

OUCH!

...TO THE COOKS.

ALL EXCEPT —

97..98.. 99....

BAH! HOW CAN I BECOME THE KING?

AND —

YUMMY! WHAT DELICIOUS LADDOOS!

OOOOOH! HOW MY TUMMY HURTS.

MUST BE ALL THOSE LADDOOS YOU ATE. THERE IS NO ESCAPING IT, YOUR MAJESTY. YOU WILL HAVE TO EXERCISE DAILY.

EXCELLENT! EXERCISES MEAN INJURED ANKLES, TORN LIGAMENTS, BETTER STILL— A BROKEN BACK! HEH! HEH!

HUFF..PUFF..THIS IS HARD WORK!

DRAT! SO MANY DAYS HAVE PASSED AND NOT A SINGLE INJURY! ALL THOSE FATTY LAYERS DO PROTECT HIM WELL!

WAIT, SIR!

WHO..WHAT? WHO IS IT?

IT'S ME, VETAL RAM.

VETAL RAM WAS THE ROYAL GARDENER.

AH! VETAL RAM, WHY DID YOU STOP ME?

LOOK HERE, SIR...

... HAD YOU FALLEN INTO THIS BIG PIT, YOU WOULD'VE SURELY BROKEN YOUR NECK.

A BIG PIT AND A BROKEN NECK EH! HEH, HEH!

?

NOT TO MENTION YOUR BROKEN NECK ONCE I PUSH YOU INTO THAT PIT.

THE NEXT DAY —

I AM SO BORED DOING THE SAME EXERCISES EVERYDAY.

WHY DON'T WE GO FOR A WALK, YOUR MAJESTY. IT WILL BE GOOD FOR YOU.

HMM.. THE FRESH AIR IS SO WONDERFUL. NO TENSION, NO PRESSURES AND NO TRAINERS!

AND NO ONE TO SEE US!!

UNKNOWN TO TANTRI, SOMEBODY WAS WATCHING.

AH! TWO HUMANS.. THE PLUMP ONE WILL LAST ME A MONTH AT LEAST! I'LL LET THE THIN ONE GO. HE LOOKS TOO NASTY TO EAT!

30

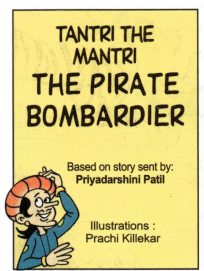

TANTRI THE MANTRI
THE PIRATE BOMBARDIER

Based on story sent by:
Priyadarshini Patil

Illustrations :
Prachi Killekar

RAJA HOOJA WAS ON HIS WAY TO SEE HIS AILING GRANDMOTHER IN SRI LANKA.

POOR GRANDMOTHER IS IN THE HOSPITAL, TANTRI. THIS SHIP SHOULD GO FASTER !

DON'T WORRY, YOUR MAJESTY. WE'LL BE THERE SOON.

TANTRI, LOOK DOWN THERE ! SILVER SHARKS !

KILLER SHARKS ? FABULOUS !

TANTRI DID NOT HAVE TO STRAIN HIS BRAIN FOR HIS NEXT PLOT. THAT NIGHT —

SHARKS ! JAWS ! HMMM

ONE LITTLE PUSH AND OFF YOU GO ...DOWN IN THE WATERSDEEP BELOW !

SUDDENLY THE CAPTAIN CAME RUSHING TO THEM.

YOUR MAJESTY, YOUR MAJESTY ! WE HAVE JUST BEEN SPOTTED BY PIRATES. THEY ARE HEADING TOWARDS OUR SHIP

?

OH NO !

HANG ON, TANTRI! SWIM TO THIS FLOAT!

SPLASH

BUT BEFORE TANTRI COULD GET TO THE FLOAT —

YIKES! A SHARK!

A CRUNCHY TANTRI CRACKER

TANTRI, WHERE ARE YOU GOING?

YAIYEE!

COME BACK, CRACKER!

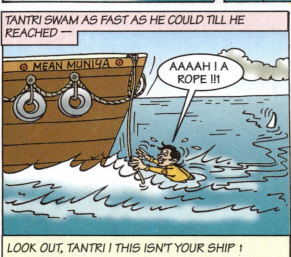

TANTRI SWAM AS FAST AS HE COULD TILL HE REACHED —

MEAN MUNIYA

AAAAH! A ROPE!!1

LOOK OUT, TANTRI! THIS ISN'T YOUR SHIP!

TANTRI HAULED HIMSELF UP BUT COULD NOT STOP RUNNING.

HELP! A SHARK!

WATCH OUT! STOP!

AND —

BOOM

AAAH!

TOPPLE

34

STRANGE. THEY SHOT THEMSELVES! WHAT BAD AIM! BUT WHERE HAS TANTRI DISAPPEARED?

JUST THEN—

YOUR MAJESTY, YOUR MAJESTY, I SAW IT ALL HAPPENING! TANTRI SWAM TO THE PIRATE SHIP AND RAN RIGHT INTO THE PIRATE WHO WAS GOING TO FIRE AT US! HE SAVED US!

WOW! WHAT A HERO! BUT HOW IS HE?

YOU MUST UNDERSTAND, YOUR MAJESTY, THAT IT WAS A VERY BIG EXPLOSION!

OH NO! MY POOR TANTRI. HE HAS GIVEN UP HIS LIFE FOR ME.

HOOJA REACHED SRI LANKA VERY DEJECTED. AT THE HOSPITAL—

HOW ARE YOU FEELING GRANDMA?

MUCH BETTER! IN FACT, I'VE BEEN COUNSELLING MY FRIEND THERE.

TANTRI! WHAT A SURPRISE! I ALWAYS KNEW MY BRAVEST MINISTER WOULD NEVER LEAVE ME.

SOME FISHERMEN PICKED HIM UP FROM THE SEA.

AAAARGH

TANTRI THE MANTRI
THE RAJA'S NEW CLOTHES

Based on a story sent by:
Pranjal Pran Saikia
Illustrations:
Prachi Killekar

TANTRI WAS RECOVERING FROM YET ANOTHER UNSUCCESSFUL ATTEMPT TO GRAB THE THRONE.

THE SKY IS GREY...THE MUD IS BROWN. WHEN, OH WHEN WILL I GET THE CROWN!

GREETINGS, TANTRI! THIS NEW INVENTION WILL SURELY HAVE YOU OUT OF BED IN NO TIME!

OH NO! KUBUDDHI WITH ANOTHER PLAN!

NEVERTHELESS TANTRI WAS CURIOUS.

WHAT IS THIS, KUBUDDHI?

A BRAND NEW SHIRT, TANTRI.

SHIRT? HAVE YOU FINALLY DECIDED TO GIVE UP SCIENCE AND INVENTION?

NO, TANTRI. THIS SHIRT IS MY NEW INVENTION. IT IS THE KUBU-ITCHY SHIRT.

ANYONE WHO WEARS THIS SHIRT WILL HAVE A BOUT OF ITCHING AND THEN FALL UNCONSCIOUS.

HMM... VERY SMART. BUT WILL IT SUIT HOOJA?

OF COURSE IT WILL, TANTRI. SPECIALLY WHEN THE ITCHING BEGINS!

HOW FUNNY HOOJA WILL LOOK! YES, I'LL TAKE THE SHIRT, KUBUDDHI.

TANTRI PAID 600 GOLD COINS FOR A KUBU-ITCHY SHIRT.

AND NOT VERY FAR AWAY, IN RAJA DOOJA'S KINGDOM —

YOUR HIGHNESS, THIS IS DR KNOW, A VERY FAMOUS SCIENTIST.

WHAT DO YOU KNOW, DR KNOW?

EVERYTHING THERE IS TO KNOW, YOUR HIGHNESS!

I KNOW THE PERFECT DISGUISE FOR FINISHING OFF RAJA HOOJA. I WILL GO AS A BEGGAR ARMED WITH MY GUN AND DO THE JOB. I WILL, I KNOW!

BUT ARE YOU SURE NOBODY WILL SUSPECT YOU?

HEE HEE ... YOU FORGET THAT I KNOW! I WILL MAKE A CONVINCING BEGGAR. I KNOW I WILL!

OR SO DR KNOW THOUGHT.

THERE ...THE GUN IS SECURE UNDER MY SHIRT. I WILL JUST PULL IT OUT AND FIRE, TAKE OFF MY DISGUISE AND ESCAPE. HEE HEE! I KNOW.

MEANWHILE, TANTRI HAD FULLY RECOVERED AND WAS ADDING FINISHING TOUCHES TO HIS PLAN.

HMM... LA LA LA! A NICE RED BOW AND THE KUBU-ITCHY SHIRT IS READY FOR ACTION.

HELLO, TANTRI. I AM SO HAPPY TO SEE YOU BACK ON YOUR FEET.

HERE IS A SMALL TOKEN OF MY RESPECT AND AFFECTION, YOUR HIGHNESS.

OOH, A GIFT FOR ME! YOU ARE SO THOUGHTFUL, TANTRI.

JUST MY FAVOURITE SHADE OF RED. I COULD WEAR IT FOR TANTRI'S WELCOME-BACK PARTY BUT MY PANTS DON'T MATCH.

JUST THEN —

SIRE, I KNOW YOU WILL HELP A POOR MAN.

UH HUH?

RAJA HOOJA WENT TO THE WINDOW.

POOR MAN... I SHOULD GIVE HIM SOMETHING.

OH NO, THE GUN IS STUCK!

HOOJA THREW THE SHIRT TO THE BEGGAR.

HERE, TAKE THIS SHIRT, MY MAN. NOBODY IN MY KINGDOM SHOULD WEAR RAGS.

DID YOU LIKE THE SHIRT, YOUR HIGHNESS?

I AM SORRY, TANTRI, I GAVE OFF THE SHIRT TO THAT BEGGAR THERE.

BUT, YOUR HIGHNESS....

FATHEAD!

OOPS... THAT'S TANTRI! HE ALWAYS SAVES HOOJA, I KNOW! I HAD BETTER GET AWAY.

AT TANTRI'S WELCOME-BACK PARTY —

EVERYONE IS SO GLAD TO SEE YOU ON YOUR FEET AGAIN, TANTRI.

NOTHING EVER GOES RIGHT!

AND JUST OUTSIDE THE PALACE DR KNOW WAS GETTING READY.

I KNOW I CANNOT FAIL THIS TIME. I KNOW THE GUN IS INSIDE THE POCKET. I KNOW THE SHIRT SUITS ME. HEE HEE!

DR KNOW WALKED INTO THE HALL WHERE THE PARTY WAS GOING ON.

I MUST STAND NEAR THIS WINDOW, FIRE AT HOOJA AND ESCAPE. I KNOW I WILL SUCCEED THIS TIME.

SUDDENLY —

HEY, THAT'S THE BEGGAR I GAVE MY SHIRT TO. IT RATHER SUITS HIM, DON'T YOU THINK, TANTRI?

WHY AM I ITCHING ALL OVER? I DON'T KNOW!

SCRATCH
SCRATCH

I WONDER WHY HE LOOKS SO TROUBLED?! LET'S GO ASK HIM, TANTRI.

THAT COULD HAVE BEEN YOU. SIGH!

HELLO THERE … ER… WHAT'S WRONG? DON'T YOU LIKE THE SHIRT? ARE YOU NOT WELL?

I DON'T KNOW! I DON'T KNOW!

SCRATCH

THE KUBU-ITCHY SHIRT TRULY LIVED UP TO ITS NAME!

I DON'T …!

HE HAS FAINTED! QUICK, LET HIM HAVE SOME AIR.

SOON, THE GUN WAS DISCOVERED.

HE MUST HAVE BEEN SENT BY RAJA DOOJA TO KILL ME.

DID HE SEND YOU?

I DON'T KNOW!

WHEN DR KNOW WAS PACKED OFF TO PRISON —

LET US CELEBRATE TANTRI'S RECOVERY AND MY NARROW ESCAPE.

ALL'S BAD THAT ENDS SAD!

39

TANTRI THE MANTRI
The Pepper Plot

Based on a story sent by:
Abir Dasgupta,

Illustrations :
Prachi Killekar

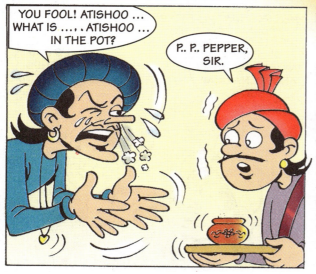

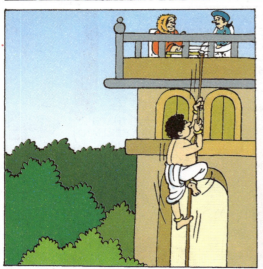

BUT THEN—

OOPS! DROPPED MY SPOON.

HERE GOES!

AAAAARGH!

ATISHOO!

ATISHOO!

ATISHOO!

ATISHOO!

ATISHOO!

THUD!

YOUR HIGHNESS! WE HAVE JUST RECEIVED INFORMATION THAT A DANGEROUS BURGLAR WILL TRY AND ENTER THE PALACE FROM THIS SIDE OF THE TERRACE.

AHA! THAT'S WHO HE WAS! YOU'LL FIND HIM DOWNSTAIRS.

TANTRI'S SWIFT ACTION SAVED THE DAY. YOU ARE A GENIUS, TANTRI!

A FAILED GENIUS. SOB!

43

TANTRI THE MANTRI in TANTRI THE KING?

Story: Reena I. Puri
Script: Janaki Viswanathan
Illustrations : Prachi Killekar

TANTRI HAD ONCE AGAIN 'SAVED' KING HOOJA'S LIFE.

THANK YOU, TANTRI... YOU REALLY SAVED ME.

YET AGAIN...MY PLEASURE, SIRE.

WHEN HOOJA LEFT —

PSST... TANTRI.

OH NO!

I HAVE DEVELOPED A NEW....

I AM NEVER GOING TO USE ANY OF YOUR INVENTIONS AGAIN. GET OUT!

SOB! I GIVE UP...I'LL NEVER EVER WEAR THE CROWN. I'LL ALWAYS REMAIN TANTRI THE MANTRI...SOB!

OVER THE NEXT FEW DAYS —

TANTRI, SHOULD I WEAR THE BLUE TURBAN OR THE PINK ONE?

YES, SIRE.

TANTRI, HAVE I PUT ON WEIGHT?

YES, SIRE.

HMM...TANTRI HAS BECOME VERY SAD AND QUIET. HE HASN'T EVEN NOTICED THAT I HAVE SLIMMED DOWN.

44

IT CAN'T BE...I AM DREAMING.

HOOJA FELL?

HOOJA FELL!

TANTRI WALKED BACK TO THE PALACE.

HUMPTY HOOJA CAUGHT THE BALL, HUMPTY HOOJA HAD A GREAT FALL! ALL THE COURTIERS WEPT AND SOBBED, AND TANTRI THE MANTRI BECAME KING AFTER ALL!

WHEN HE REACHED THE PALACE GATES —

A GREAT TRAGEDY HAS OCCURRED (SOB!) RAJA HOOJA... RAJA HOOJA (SOB!) FELL FROM TIGI HILLS!

W... WHAT ?

NO !

THE WHOLE KINGDOM WAS IN SHOCK. AS FOR TANTRI —

HMM...I MUST MOURN THE WHOLE DAY TODAY. THEN IN THE EVENING I CAN PROCLAIM MYSELF AS THE NEW KING.

HE SUMMONED HIS ASSISTANT.

EVERYBODY MUST WEAR WHITE. SUMMON ALL THE COURTIERS TO THE ROYAL COURT. OUR DEAREST RAJA DESERVES A ROYAL MOURNING.

YES, SIRE.

47

TANTRI THE MANTRI
The Laddoo Story

Story: Aashish Jindal
Script: Janaki Viswanathan
Illustrations: Prachi Killekar

49

TANTRI RESORTED TO SIGN LANGUAGE.

YOU SEE THIS BOTTLE?

HMMM.

???

MAKE SOME LADDOOS... PUT THIS IN THEM.

HMM.

DID YOU UNDERSTAND?

YES, YES. I HAVE TO PUT THIS POTION IN IT, I UNDERSTOOD. IS IT FOR HEALTH REASONS?

Y...YES. IT WILL GIVE THE KING A LONG LIFE.

YOUR WIFE? SHE IS IN THE PALACE GARDENS, SIR.

GRRR! GET THIS MAN OUT OF MY SIGHT.

YOU MAY GO.

JUST BEFORE LUNCH, TANTRI RUSHED TO THE ROYAL KITCHEN.

I HAVE PUT THE LOTION LIKE YOU TOLD ME TO, SIR.

REALLY? YIPPEE! I'LL GO MAKE FAT FACE EAT ONE RIGHT NOW!

YOUR HIGHNESS, PLEASE BEGIN THE MEAL ON A SWEET NOTE. HAVE A LADDOO.

THANK YOU, MY DEAR TANTRI. HERE, HAVE THE POTATO SALAD. YOU LIKE IT VERY MUCH, DON'T YOU?

50

JUST THEN —

HMM... DELICIOUS!

MR TANTRI, I NEED TO SPEAK WITH YOU URGENTLY.

NO, NOT NOW, LATER. I AM BUSY.

IT IS A MATTER OF LIFE AND DEATH. PLEASE, SIR!

FOOL! I DIDN'T WANT TO MISS SEEING FAT FACE WHEN THE POISON TOOK EFFECT.

TANTRI FOLLOWED VICHITRABUDDHI OUTSIDE THE DINING HALL.

SIGH...TO LEAVE THE WORLD AT SUCH A YOUNG AGE!

DON'T TELL ME YOU'RE FEELING SORRY FOR HOOJA?!

OWW! MY STOMACH IS HURTING! IT MUST BE INDIGESTION. HURRY UP AND TELL ME WHAT IT IS.

IF ONLY IT WERE THAT SIMPLE... SIGH! WHAT ACTUALLY HAPPENED WAS...

...THE COOK PUT IN THE POISON AS YOU ASKED HIM TO. ONLY, HE HEARD '*ALOO' INSTEAD OF LADDOO. AND YOU HAVE JUST EATEN THE POTATO SALAD ...SOB!

GROAN! OWW!

AND LIKE ALWAYS —

CHEER UP, TANTRI. HERE, HAVE A LADDOO. THE COOK MADE THEM ESPECIALLY FOR YOU.

LADDOO?! EEEYAAA!

* POTATO

51

TANTRI THE MANTRI
Tantri and the Bees

Based on a story sent by:
Aravind Bhangale,

Illustrations: Prachi Killekar

IF HE EATS ALL THAT, I WON'T HAVE TO DO ANYTHING. HE'LL EXPLODE BY HIMSELF! ANYWAY, NOW'S MY CHANCE TO SLIP AWAY!

WAITING FOR HIM OUTSIDE IS —

VICHITRABUDDHI!

AT YOUR SERVICE!

TANTRI, I HAVE A FOOLPROOF PLAN TO GET RID OF HOOJA!

A FOOLPROOF PLAN? ALL YOUR PLANS HAVE FAILED SO FAR!

THIS FRUIT WILL DO THE TRICK! IT ATTRACTS BEES IN THEIR HUNDREDS!

GIVE IT TO HOOJA AND TAKE HIM TO THE GARDEN...

...HE'LL BE STUNG TO DEATH! BRILLIANT!

TANTRI THOUGHT HARD.

I CAN'T GIVE HOOJA THE FRUIT. HE'LL EAT IT BEFORE A SINGLE BEE CAN GET A SNIFF AT IT!

I KNOW! I'LL BUY HIM A TURBAN AND HIDE THE FRUIT INSIDE IT!

TANTRI BOUGHT AN ELABORATE TURBAN.

DON'T TELL ME YOU'VE BOUGHT ANOTHER TURBAN! YOU'VE GOT A BEE IN YOUR BONNET ABOUT TURBANS!

THERE WILL CERTAINLY BE MANY BEES IN THIS BONNET…ER… TURBAN!

ON CORONATION DAY –

HERE'S A LITTLE GIFT TO CELEBRATE YOUR REIGN, RAJA HOOJA!

WHY, TANTRI! IT'S BEAUTIFUL!

HOW DO I LOOK IN IT?

MAGNIFICENT, YOUR MAJESTY!

I'M SURE THE BEES WILL THINK SO TOO!

ER…I'VE ARRANGED A SURPRISE FOR YOU IN THE GARDEN BEFORE YOUR PARTY.

YOU'VE BEEN AS BUSY AS A BEE, HAVEN'T YOU, TANTRI?

TANTRI THE MANTRI
Third Time Unlucky

Story: Jubel D'Cruz
Script: Janaki Viswanathan
Illustrations: Prachi Killekar

TANTRI, THERE IS A PACKAGE FOR YOU IN THE POST.

YES! IT MUST HAVE COME!

OOH! IT LOOKS JUST LIKE A REGULAR MOBILE PHONE. WHO WOULD GUESS THAT IT HIDES THE MOST DEADLY BOMB!

THIRD TIME UNLUCKY MOBILE PHONE! MAKE ONE CALL AND TALK ...MAKE THE SECOND CALL AND TALK. BUT MAKE THE THIRD CALL AND...BOOM! THE BOMB EXPLODES EXACTLY 10 SECONDS INTO THE THIRD CALL. GOOD LUCK! OR SHOULD WE SAY...BAD LUCK?!

- KHATARNAAK & CO.

GREAT! ALL I HAVE TO DO IS GIVE THIS TO FAT-FACE AND THEN...!

TANTRI, WHERE ARE YOU GOING? WHAT'S IN THAT PACKAGE?

IT'S THE THIRD TIME UNLUCKY MOBILE PHONE!

OH! BY KHATARNAAK & CO? IT HAS A HIGH SUCCESS RATIO. BUT CAN I GIVE YOU ONE TIP?

NO, THANKS. THE KING'S HERE.

TANTRI, THERE YOU ARE!

YOUR FAT... HIGHNESS!

TANTRI, THE SAVIOUR

Story: Savio & Gayathri
Script: Janaki Viswanathan
Illustrations: Prachi Killekar

I THINK YOU SHOULD STAY OUT OF THE PALACE TODAY.

WHY?

BECAUSE IF YOU'RE AROUND HOOJA, EVERY PLAN BACKFIRES AND YOU END UP IN HOSPITAL.

HMMM. YOU HAVE A POINT. BUT AT LEAST TELL ME WHAT YOU'VE PLANNED FOR HIM!

NO! BUT I GUARANTEE YOU, IT'S ONE DEADLY PACKAGE!

HEH HEH! OKAY, DUSHTA, I'LL GO HOME.

AND I WANT GOOD NEWS AT THE END OF THE DAY!

YOU'LL HAVE IT!

MEANWHILE IN TANTRI'S HOUSE—

THE STARS SAY MANY THINGS...SOMETIMES GOOD, SOMETIMES BAD, AND...

...SOMETIMES... UGLY!

TANTRI! COME LISTEN! THE ROYAL ASTROLOGER IS READING OUR FORECASTS FOR THIS WEEK.

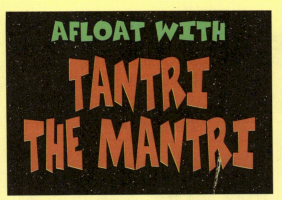

AFLOAT WITH
TANTRI THE MANTRI

TANTRI THE MANTRI IS TAKING RAJA HOOJA FOR A RIDE. LOOK AT THE TWO PICTURES CAREFULLY. ALTHOUGH THE TWO SCENES SEEM TO BE IDENTICAL, THERE ARE SOME DIFFERENCES. CAN YOU SPOT 7 DIFFERENCES BETWEEN THE TWO PICTURES?

It'll be easier to find the differences if you colour the pictures!

TANTRI THE MANTRI
IN
WINDY MOUNTAIN

By: Luis Fernandes
Illustrations: Prachi Killekar

68

69

IT'S A LONG AND ARDUOUS CLIMB, BUT FINALLY —

WELL, HERE WE ARE.

(PUFF)... (GASP)....

HEY, WHAT ABOUT THE RETURN JOURNEY?

NOBODY EVER RETURNS! GOOD LUCK, SIR!!

I'D BETTER NOT STAY TOO LONG, EITHER!

HOOJA'S GONE TO THE EDGE! GOOD! I WON'T WAIT FOR THE WINDS!!

I SAY, TANTRI. COME HERE. WHAT A VIEW!!

HEY!

HE'S GONE! IT WAS EASIER THAN I EXPECTED!!

I'VE GOT RID OF HIM AT LAST! I'VE WAITED SO LONG FOR THIS!!! NOW THE THRONE IS....

71